W9-CDZ-995

ALL ABOUT

Earth and SPACE

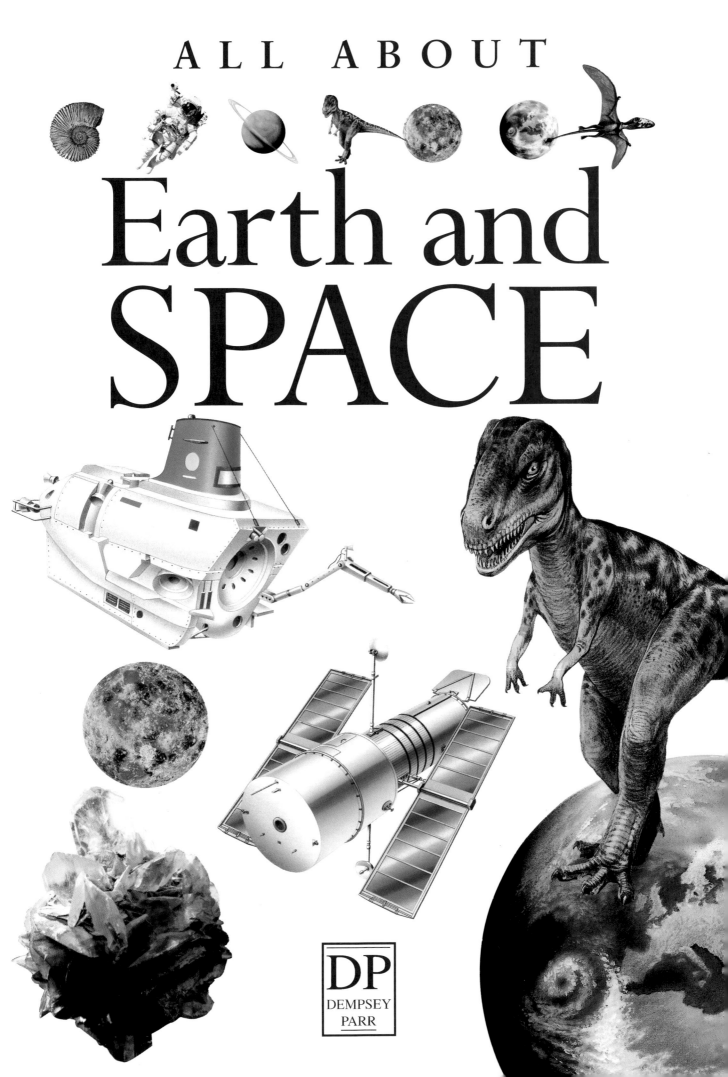

ALL ABOUT
Earth and
SPACE

DP
DEMPSEY
PARR

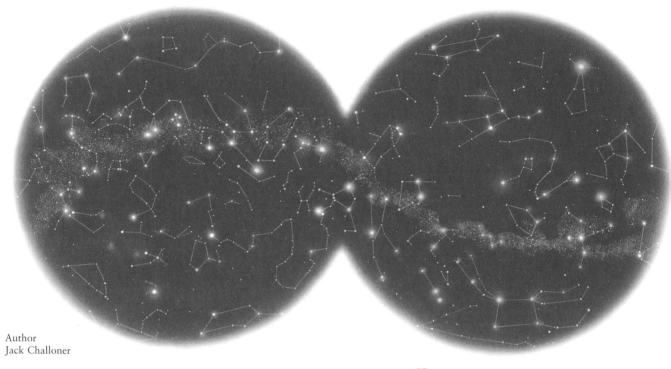

Author
Jack Challoner

Designers
Diane Clouting and Phil Kay

Editor
Linda Sonntag

Project Management
Raje Airey and Liz Dalby

Artwork Commissioning
Susanne Grant

Picture Research
Janice Bracken and Kate Miles

Additional editorial help from
Lesley Cartlidge, Jenni Cozens, Libbe Mella,
and Ian Paulyn

Editorial Director
Paula Borton

Art Director
Clare Sleven

Director
Jim Miles

First published in 1999 by
Dempsey Parr
Dempsey Parr is an imprint of Parragon
Parragon, Queen Street House, 4 Queen Street, Bath, BA1 1HE, UK

Copyright © Parragon 1999

Produced by Miles Kelly Publishing Ltd
Bardfield Centre, Great Bardfield, Essex, England CM7 4SL

All rights reserved. No part of this publication may be reproduced, stored
in a retrieval system, or transmitted by any means, electronic, mechanical,
photocopying, recording, or otherwise, without the prior permission of
the copyright holder.

ISBN 1-84084-455-8 (Hardback)
ISBN 1-84084-476-0 (Paperback)

Printed in Italy

CONTENTS

EARTH AND SPACE

ALL ABOUT EARTH AND SPACE is divided
into fifteen different topics, each covered
by a double-page spread. On every spread,
you can find some or all of the following:

● Main text to introduce the topic

● The main illustration, designed to inform
  about an important aspect of the topic

● Smaller illustrations with captions, to
  describe aspects of the topic in detail

● Photographs of unusual or specialized
  subjects

● Fact boxes and charts, containing
  interesting nuggets of information

● Biography boxes, about the scientists
  who have helped us to understand the
  way the Universe works

● Projects and activities

THE UNIVERSE

WHEN YOU LOOK UP at the sky on a clear night, you are looking out into the Universe. Most of the Universe is just a vast ocean of empty space. But there are islands in the ocean, called galaxies. A galaxy is a huge group of stars, millions of millions of miles across. Each star is a huge ball of hot glowing gas like our Sun, only much farther away. Each star that we can see from Earth is in our galaxy, which is called the Milky Way. The Universe contains billions of galaxies. You may have wondered where the Universe came from. Most astronomers are convinced that it all started as a tiny, very hot ball about 15 billion years ago. Astronomers believe that in a kind of explosion called the Big Bang, the ball expanded (grew) rapidly, like a balloon being blown up.

In the beginning...

If the Universe really did begin with a Big Bang, then the galaxies in space should still be moving away from each other, like debris thrown out in all directions from an explosion. And this is what astronomers have found—that every galaxy, in every direction, is moving away from us.

Barred spiral galaxy

Elliptical galaxy

Galaxy shapes

Maybe one day humans will travel out of our galaxy and look back at it. If they do, they will see a huge, slowly spinning white spiral-shaped disc. Many galaxies are spirals like this, but others are egg-shaped (elliptical). A third type of galaxy, irregular, has no regular shape at all.

Spiral galaxy

You are here!

Our nearest star is the Sun. Our planet, Earth, travels around the Sun at a distance of about 95 million miles. The next nearest star, Proxima Centauri, lies at a distance of about 25 million million miles – nearly 300,000 times as far. Light that reaches Earth from Proxima Centauri has travelled for four years. An astronomer would say that Proxima Centauri is four light years away. The Sun and Proxima Centauri are both part of our galaxy, the Milky Way. It is about 100,000 light years across. The distance to the next galaxy is about two million light years. Light from the most distant galaxies, at the edge of the known Universe, takes about 10 billion years to reach us.

The nine planets of the solar system orbit the Sun (above, right). Nearest to the Sun is Mercury, followed by Venus, Earth, Mars, Jupiter, Saturn, Uranus, Neptune, and Pluto

A star is born

Stars form in huge clouds of gas and dust inside galaxies. These clouds are called nebulae (singular "nebula"), from the Greek word "nephos," which means "cloud."

What is a star?

The Milky Way galaxy contains about 100 billion of them. A star is a huge ball of hot gas—the Sun is more than 600,000 miles across, for example—more than a 75 times the width of the Earth. Its high temperature means that it glows, just as the element of an electric toaster glows when it is hot, although the Sun is much hotter than a toaster. When a star comes to the end of its life, it may just cool down and stop shining. Some stars explode at the end of their lives in spectacular explosions called supernovas. The largest stars shrink at the end of their lives to become very strange objects called black holes, which can swallow whole stars without growing in size.

Young hot stars

This photograph, which was taken through a telescope, shows a group, or cluster, of stars. They are all hot young stars that have formed from the same nebula, which looks like a blue and pink cloud. Some nebulae are visible to the naked eye as small fuzzy patches of light.

Holes in space

Some stars become bizarre objects called black holes when they reach the end of their lifetimes. Objects—and even light—anywhere near a black hole are pulled into the hole by a strong gravitational force. Once inside, any material object is stretched and squashed out of existence. Time runs more slowly near a black hole, and stops altogether inside it.

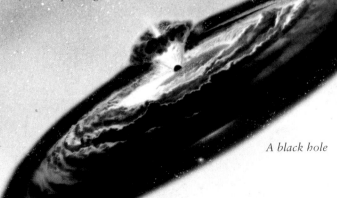

A black hole

LOOKING AT THE STARS

On a dark, clear winter's night, you can see the heart of our galaxy with the naked eye. It is a hazy white band across the sky, which is why it is called the Milky Way. Now find the constellation of Andromeda using a star map. On a clear dark night, it appears as a hazy patch of light. At more than two million light years away, it is the most distant object visible to the naked eye. If you live in the southern hemisphere, try to see the Large and Small Magellanic Clouds: they are "small" nearby galaxies. All these things look much more spectacular through binoculars. See if you can borrow some.

ASTRONOMY

ASTRONOMY IS THE STUDY of the stars, planets, and other objects in space. You can see stars, the Moon, some of the planets and the Sun using just your eyes, but a telescope gives a much better view. The telescope was invented about 400 years ago, but astronomy is much older than this. Ancient astronomers in China and Greece could predict when certain events such as eclipses would take place. The ancient astronomers identified patterns in the stars, which they called constellations. They thought that the patterns were pictures of characters from their myths and legends, so they have names such as "Taurus, the Bull" and "Ursa Major, the Great Bear." Modern astronomers still think of the stars in constellations, but only for the purpose of identifying stars. Today's astronomers use telescopes that detect radio waves and other rays, as well as light, coming from outer space. They can even study stars and planets using remote-controlled telescopes in space.

Astrolabe
The ancient astronomers used complicated devices like this astrolabe to follow the motions of the stars, the planets, the Moon, and the Sun across the sky. Today, astronomers track the stars using sophisticated computers and extremely powerful telescopes.

GALILEO
Italian scientist Galileo Galilei was born in Pisa in 1564. He first looked at the night sky through a telescope in 1609, and described the craters on the Moon, the moons of Jupiter, and the millions of stars in the Milky Way. He was put in jail by the Catholic Church for suggesting that the Earth orbits the Sun.

A map of the sky
Looking up at the night sky, the stars appear to be painted on a great dome. These two sky-maps show a flattened-out version of the night sky as seen in the southern and northern hemispheres. Which stars you see on a certain night depends on your latitude, the time of year, the time of night, and, of course, the weather. At the center of the northern sky is Polaris, the North Star, which appears to remain above the North Pole.

MAKE A TELESCOPE

You can see how a telescope works, using a magnifying glass and an eye glass lens. Hold the magnifying glass at arm's length and hold the other lens about 2 inches in front of your eyes. Move both lenses nearer or farther from your eyes until you can see a clear image. The object will not look much closer than you see it with your eyes. The specially designed lenses in a refracting telescope can make things look much closer than the lenses you have used.

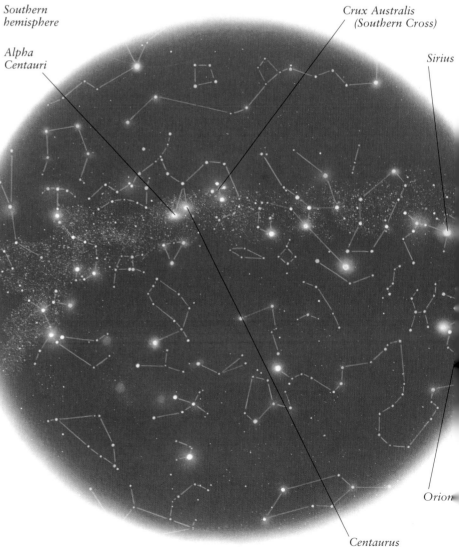

Southern hemisphere

Alpha Centauri

Crux Australis (Southern Cross)

Sirius

Centaurus

Orion

Telescopes

Most telescopes contain lenses and mirrors that allow astronomers to see objects in space much larger and brighter than they appear to the naked eye. You may have looked through a pair of binoculars, which work in the same way. Light from a distant object passes through a lens, or reflects off a mirror and is focused by a lens, to form an image of the object in your eye. The larger the lens or the mirror, the more light the telescope collects and the brighter the image will be. Not all telescopes use light to form images, however. A radio telescope, for example, produces pictures of distant stars and galaxies from the radio waves they give out. There are also telescopes that can form images by detecting infrared, ultraviolet, and X-rays.

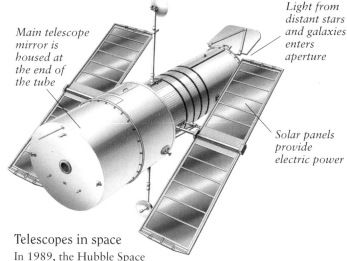

Main telescope mirror is housed at the end of the tube

Light from distant stars and galaxies enters aperture

Solar panels provide electric power

The southern hemisphere

The constellations of the southern skies were given names by the European explorers of the 17th and 18th centuries. Among them are Centaurus, the centaur, a beast that is half-man and half-horse. This contains the nearest star system in the sky, Alpha Centauri, 4.3 light years away. Below Centaurus are the spectacular stars of the Southern Cross, which guided the navigators of the past.

Telescopes in space

In 1989, the Hubble Space Telescope was launched by the Space Shuttle. Because the telescope is above the Earth's atmosphere, it can get a better view of the stars than a telescope on the ground. There are telescopes in space that detect infrared and X-ray radiation as well as light.

Astronomers at work

Most modern astronomers work in buildings called observatories. The domed roof of this observatory slides open, so that the telescope can be directed to any point in the night sky.

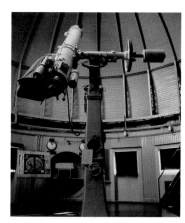

Northern Hemisphere

Polaris

Ground-based observatory (above) and photograph taken by space telescope (below).

Come closer...

A telescope can make things look closer than they are. You can see craters and mountains on our Moon, and the moons of planet Jupiter, for example. Telescopes with only lenses are called refracting telescopes, while those that use mirrors are called reflecting telescopes. This photograph of the birth of a star was taken by the Hubble Space Telescope.

THE SOLAR SYSTEM

YOU ARE LIVING ON one of nine planets that together with their moons, the Sun, and millions of chunks of rock and ice make up what is known as the Solar System. The chunks of rock and ice are called comets, asteroids, and meteoroids. Comets have been described as "dirty snowballs," which is accurate, except that they are probably made of rock at the center. There are millions of asteroids, the largest of which is about 600 miles in diameter. Meteoroids are small pieces of debris left over from the formation of the Solar System some 4.5 billion years ago. Every day, tons of meteoroids enter the Earth's atmosphere at high speed. Friction with the air heats the meteoroids to white hot, and most vaporize completely in an eye-catching display known as a meteor, or shooting star. The Sun sits at the center of the Solar System. The other objects, including our own planet, Earth, move around the Sun in paths called orbits.

The Sun and planets

Each of the inner planets, including Earth, is made mainly of solid rock, and has a molten core. The outer planets, except Pluto, are called "gas giants," because they consist almost entirely of gas. If you could weigh the objects of the Solar System, you would find that the Sun would weigh more than everything else put together.

Venus is about the same size as Earth. Its thick atmosphere traps the Sun's heat, so the planet is very hot

Mercury is the closest planet to the Sun. It is too hot and too small to have an atmosphere

Sun

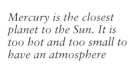

Orbits

The closer a planet is to the Sun, the less time it takes to complete each orbit. So, while the Earth takes one year, Venus, which is closer to the Sun, takes less than five months. Orbits are shaped like slightly flattened circles called ellipses. All the bodies of the Solar System are held in orbit around the Sun by the force of gravity. Gravitational attraction between the Sun and the Earth is what stops the Earth moving off in a straight line, out of the Solar System. Just as the Earth orbits the Sun, the Moon orbits the Earth, and there are moons orbiting most of the other planets.

Jupiter is by far the largest of the planets. A large red spot on its surface is a huge storm, bigger than the whole of the Earth

Mars is known as the red planet. This is because of the abundance of a chemical compound called iron oxide in its rocks and soil

Earth is the only planet we know to have life. Its atmosphere is rich in oxygen, and there is plenty of liquid water on its surface

Inner planets

The four rocky innermost planets and their moons have marks on their surfaces called craters. These are the result of millions of years of bombardment by meteoroids. On Earth and Venus, many of these craters are covered over by molten rock that escapes from beneath the surface.

Our star

At the center of the Solar System is our star, the Sun, a huge ball of very hot gas that has more than 100 times the diameter of the Earth. The temperature at its center is around 27 million degrees Fahrenheit, and heat flows outward in all directions to the surface.

Infrared

This photograph of the Sun (left), taken using a camera sensitive to infrared radiation, shows how active the surface of the Sun is. You can clearly see solar prominence, a gigantic plume of gas shooting up from the surface.

Gas giants

The planets Jupiter, Saturn, Uranus, and Neptune are made mainly of gases, though their cores are liquid and in some cases probably solid. High-speed winds swirl different colored bands of gas around these planets, making them look like polished marbles.

Uranus and Neptune orbit at huge distances from the Sun. They are cold, lifeless gas giants

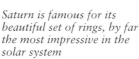

Pluto, with its moon, Charon

Saturn is famous for its beautiful set of rings, by far the most impressive in the solar system

Neptune

Odd one out

Planet Pluto is unlike the other outer planets. It is made of rock, unlike the gas giants, and is much smaller than they are. It has an unusual orbit, which for some of the time brings it closer to the Sun than Neptune. Pluto is orbited by its own moon, Charon.

Long-tailed visitor

Comets spend most of their time very far from the Sun. When a comet comes close to the Sun (within a few hundred million miles), clouds of gas, ice and dust are thrown off it, forming long tails that can be seen from the Earth.

Shooting stars

Most meteoroids are very small—the size of a speck of dust. Even they can produce a spectacular display when they hit the Earth's atmosphere. Larger meteoroids survive the journey to Earth and once they land they are called meteorites. Only about 3,000 meteorites have ever been found.

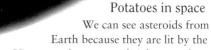
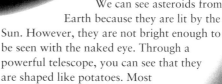

GLOSSARY

● Degree Fahrenheit (°F)—a unit of temperature. Normal human body temperature is about 98.6°F, and water normally boils at 212°F.

● Gravitational attraction—a force between any two objects that pulls them together.

● Molten—another word for liquid, most often used when describing a substance that is normally solid, such as rock or metal.

● White hot—hot enough to glow with a bright white light. The filament of an incandescent light bulb glows white hot.

● Infrared—a type of radiation like light that is invisible to human eyes, although some animals and some camera films are capable of detecting it.

Potatoes in space

We can see asteroids from Earth because they are lit by the Sun. However, they are not bright enough to be seen with the naked eye. Through a powerful telescope, you can see that they are shaped like potatoes. Most asteroids orbit the Sun between the orbits of Mars and Jupiter.

SPACE EXPLORATION

WHEN YOU LET GO of an inflated balloon, air rushes out of the nozzle and pushes the balloon in the opposite direction. Huge rockets that take satellites, space probes, and even people into space work in a similar way, except that it is hot exhaust gases, and not air, that escapes. Rockets have taken astronauts into orbit around the Earth, and to the Moon. Satellites that give us a good view of the weather, or enable people to talk to each other across the world, are also launched into orbit by rockets. Rockets were invented nearly 1,000 years ago in China, where they were used as fireworks and weapons. However, it is only in the past hundred years or so that people have thought seriously about the role of rockets in space travel. Only as recently as 1958 was the first satellite launched, and a person first walked on the Moon as recently as 1969. What might space exploration bring us in the next hundred years?

Reaching out
The first ever object that humans put into space was a satellite called Sputnik. It was launched on October 4, 1958, and it orbited the Earth for 92 days, and then burned up as it reentered the atmosphere.

Up and away
A powerful engine lifts the rocket and its payload, and speeds it up to make it reach escape velocity (see above, right). The payload may be a satellite, a space probe, or a spacecraft with people aboard. This picture shows the US Space Shuttle, a "reusable" space vehicle.

One small step...
In July 1969, American astronaut Neil Armstrong became the first person ever to stand on the Moon. As he stepped down from the spacecraft, Armstrong spoke the now famous words: "That's one small step for a man, one giant leap for mankind."

SPACE FACTS

- The first telecommunications satellite relaying telephone and television signals was Telstar, launched in 1962.
- The Space Shuttle was launched in 1982 and there have been more than 70 missions since then.
- Some experts believe that a person will walk on the planet Mars by 2010.

Rocket engines

Inside the engines of most rockets, liquid fuel burns with liquid oxygen, producing huge amounts of hot gas. The gas can escape only through the nozzle at the bottom of the engine, so it is forced downward. This pushes the rocket in the opposite direction—upward —with a great force, or thrust. In order to escape the Earth's gravitational pull and not to crash back to Earth, a rocket must reach a speed of about 24,000 miles per hour. This is called escape velocity. At this speed, the rocket travels more than 6 miles every second! The job of rocket engines does not end when a spacecraft clears the Earth's upper atmosphere. Smaller rocket engines, or retro rockets, are used to steer craft as they move through space.

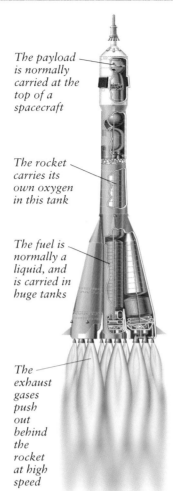

The payload is normally carried at the top of a spacecraft

The rocket carries its own oxygen in this tank

The fuel is normally a liquid, and is carried in huge tanks

The exhaust gases push out behind the rocket at high speed

Into the future

Traveling to the nearest star will take hundreds or even thousands of years. To get there as quickly as possible, future spacecraft may have engines powered by nuclear fusion. These would be able to reach much higher speeds than today's spacecraft.

Probing space

We have explored distant planets, their moons, and also the Sun, comets and asteroids— without ever visiting them. Unmanned spacecraft called probes carry cameras and other equipment, and send back pictures and other data to Earth as radio signals. The Cassini-Huygens probe (right) is in orbit around Saturn.

Looking down

Satellites orbit the Earth. Some of them help us to learn more about our world. From their position high above ground, they produce photographs and make measurements that would be impossible to make from the ground. Other satellites help with weather forecasting (above left) and relay telephone and television signals (above right) around the world.

Is anybody there?

The first object made by people to leave the Solar System was the space probe Pioneer 10. Launched in 1972, it flew past the planets Jupiter and Saturn, and passed outside Pluto's orbit some 17 years later. Aboard is this plaque carrying information about our world.

MAKE A BALLOON ROCKET

You can make a balloon rocket go in a straight line using string, sticky tape, and a drinking straw. Blow up a long straight balloon, and clip the nozzle closed with a hair clip or a bulldog clip. Cut a piece of straw about an inch long and tape it to the balloon. Feed a long piece of string through the straw and attach one end to a chair. Now, hold the balloon at the other end of the string, near to the ground, and release the clip. The balloon will shoot up the string toward the chair.

EARTH IN SPACE

IMAGINE HOLDING A BALL in a dark room and shining a flashlight at it. Half of the ball would be lit up and half would be in darkness. In the same way, the Sun lights up only half the Earth—when you are in daylight, it is night for the people on the opposite side of the Earth. The Earth spins as it moves through space, once every 24 hours, and this explains why we have day and night. Other measurements of time are also determined by the Earth's position in space. For example, a year is the length of time it takes for the Earth to complete each lap of its orbit around the Sun. Similarly, the Moon travels around the Earth, taking about a month on each circuit. During that time, the shape of the Moon varies from a thin crescent to a full circle. Sometimes, the Moon moves between the Sun and the Earth, blocking our view of the Sun. This is a solar eclipse.

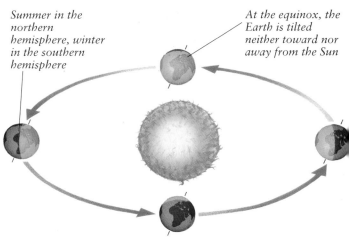

Summer in the northern hemisphere, winter in the southern hemisphere

At the equinox, the Earth is tilted neither toward nor away from the Sun

The seasons

As you can see from the picture, the Earth is tilted slightly in space. This causes the seasons. In June, for example, the North Pole points toward the Sun, so it is warmer in the northern hemisphere than in the southern hemisphere. In December, it is winter in the northern hemisphere and summer in the southern hemisphere. During summer, daytime is longer than nighttime. During winter, it is the other way around. There are two times in the year—called equinoxes—when daytime and nighttime are of equal lengths, all round the world.

Moon blocks the Sun during a solar eclipse

Blocking the Sun

In a total solar eclipse, the Moon passes in front of the Sun, blocking it completely for a few minutes, and darkness falls. A partial eclipse is when the Moon passes in front of the Sun but covers only part of it.

Day and night

You may find the view of Earth from space surprising. In this photograph, there is a line dividing the parts of the world where it is day and those where it is night. As the Earth spins, the people in the dark move into the light, and those in the light move into the dark. The Moon is in the foreground. It is also in half-shadow, and it too has daytime and nighttime. One "Moon day" lasts more than 20 "Earth days."

MAKE A SUNDIAL

It is easy to track the Sun's movement across the sky by recording the shadow of a stick at various times during the day. On a sunny day, push a long (3 foot) stick into the ground. Choose somewhere that will not be in shadow at all during the day. The stick casts a shadow, forming a dark line on the ground opposite the Sun. Place a small stone at the end of the shadow. Do the same each hour for a few hours, and you will have a record of how the Sun has moved. The next day, the shadows will move in the same way. Can you tell the time from where the shadow falls at any time of the day?

Our changing Moon

As the Moon moves around the Earth, different amounts of its lit half are visible to us. The different views of the half-lit Moon that we get during its path around us are the Moon's phases. You can see how this works in the diagram (above).

Moon shapes

When people are asked to draw a picture of the Moon, they most often draw it as a crescent shape. But the crescent is just one of the Moon's shapes, or phases. We only see the Moon at all because the Sun lights it up. Just like the Earth, only half of the Moon is lit up. As the Moon moves around the Earth, we see different amounts of the lit half. At one point of the Moon's orbit we can see none of its lit side. This is called new moon. At a different point of the orbit we can see the whole of the lit side. This is full moon. In between are the other phases of the Moon.

The shadow of the Earth

Occasionally, the Moon seems to disappear from the sky. It doesn't really disappear: the Earth blocks light from the Sun, so we can't see it. These occasions, when the shadow of the Earth falls on the Moon, are called lunar eclipses.

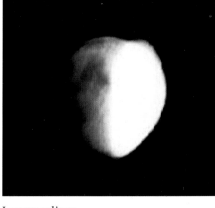

Lunar eclipse

During a lunar eclipse, the size of the shadow on the moon constantly changes, as the Earth moves.

KEY FACTS

- The Earth spins around once every 24 hours.
- The Earth takes one year to orbit the Sun.
- The Moon takes one month to orbit the Earth.
- The different shapes that the Moon has are called its phases.
- During a solar eclipse, the Moon passes in front of the Sun.
- The Sun lights up half the Earth.
- The seasons occur because the Earth is tilted.
- Other planets besides the Earth have moons.

EARTH AND CONTINENTS

OUR PLANET IS NOT AS SOLID as you might think. The ground beneath your feet seems static and stationary, but the Earth's surface actually consists of about ten sections, or plates, that are moving very slowly. These "tectonic plates" are a little like pieces of a cracked eggshell. The Earth's solid outer layer is called the crust, and it contains a wide variety of materials that people, plants, and animals need. The layer beneath the crust is called the mantle, and is made up of rock that is so incredibly hot that it is partly molten (liquid). The movement of this liquid rock shifts the tectonic plates of the crust, a bit like groceries on a conveyer belt at a supermarket checkout. As the plates collide and the crust crumples up under the enormous pressure, mountains form over millions of years. The rocks of the crust contain hidden secrets of Earth's history. Geologists—people who study rocks and minerals—have discovered some of these secrets, and have worked out that Earth was formed around 4.5 billion years ago.

EARTH FACTS
● The Earth is 7,909 miles in diameter at the equator.
● The diameter at the poles is 7,507 miles.
● The average depth of the crust is 22 miles.
● The inner core is about 1,500 miles in diameter.
● Electric currents in the metallic core produce the Earth's magnetic field.

Down to the core

There is no easy way to take samples from the center of the Earth, some 3,600 miles beneath you. Instead, geologists study how sounds travel through the Earth—from one side of the planet to the other—to try and work out the kind of materials that exist there. They need to use their imagination as well as their surveys to build up a picture of what has never been seen. The center of the Earth is called the core, and it is a ball made up of two different parts. The outer core consists of melted metals so it is obviously very hot. Surprisingly, the inner core stays solid despite being even hotter. It is, in fact, the hottest part of the entire planet, but is prevented from becoming liquid because of the great pressure.

Surface of Earth holds water in seas and lakes

The atmosphere surrounds the entire planet

Plates do not move smoothly. For most of the time, their edges are jammed together. But gradually the currents under the plates build up increasing pressure. Finally the plates move in a sharp jerk. This sudden movement shakes all the rocks around it, setting off an earthquake

What's inside?

The Earth is a huge ball, but unlike a tennis ball it is not filled with air. Its core is made mainly of liquid and solid metals, and is surrounded by the mantle, which consists of semi-liquid rock. The solid crust of the Earth is like the skin that forms when a hot bowl of oatmeal begins to cool. The Earth is more than 7,000 miles across, but the crust is no more than 22 miles thick. This relatively thin outer coating is made up of plates, as you can see from the map, right.

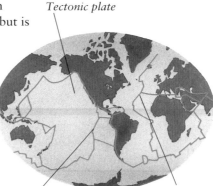
Tectonic plate

Plate boundary

Mid-Atlantic Ridge

Where plates part company...

In some parts of the Earth's crust, two neighboring plates are moving apart. Ridges of rock form between the plates, and some of these can be seen from space. The satellite photo (left) shows the Mid-Atlantic ridge that runs for thousands of miles along the floor of the Atlantic Ocean.

Breaking apart

A solid part of the crust can fall into the gap between two plates that are moving apart. That can happen on land and under the sea. It has happened in Africa, to form the Great Rift Valley (left), which is hundreds of miles long. The floor of the valley is very flat, and lies about half a mile below the surrounding land.

Finding your way

For hundreds of years, people have used magnetic compasses to find their way around. The compass needle is a small magnet that lines up with the Earth's magnetic field, which is aligned north–south wherever you are on Earth. The Earth's magnetic field is produced by strong electric currents within the core.

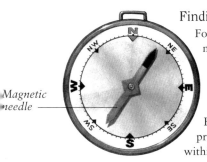

Magnetic needle

Magnetic field lines

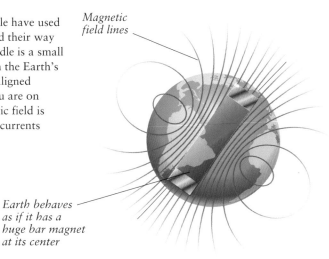

Earth behaves as if it has a huge bar magnet at its center

Relatively thin, solid crust

Mantle of molten rock

Hot outer core of molten iron, nickel, and other minerals

Inner core of hot but solid iron

Folding up

The different layers in these sandstone formations were once flat, laid down one on top of the other. They have been folded by the enormous force of two tectonic plates being pushed together. Geologists can tell much about the Earth by studying these folds, called synclines and anticlines.

A moving experience

As the tectonic plates of the Earth's crust slowly move around on the mantle, they carry the continents with them. Geologists have worked out how the continents looked millions of years ago and made a world map of the ancient past.

280 million years ago

180 million years ago

65 million years ago

Where plates collide...

There are two types of crust: oceanic crust, which forms the floor of the deep ocean, and continental crust, which forms the land. When a plate of oceanic crust collides with one made of continental crust, the oceanic crust is always forced downward. This is called a subduction zone.

Magma pushes through crust

Plates move apart

Subduction zone

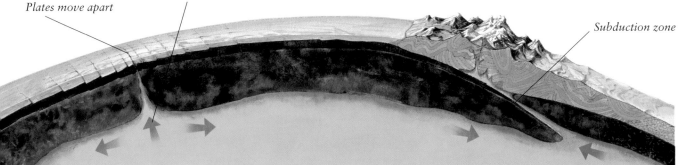

Plume of smoke accompanies an erupting volcano

The cone grows each time the volcano erupts, as more lava solidifies

EARTHQUAKES AND VOLCANOES

THE FIREWORKS OF A VOLCANO and the trembling of the earth during an earthquake are two of the most dramatic and terrifying happenings on our planet. They are both caused by the slow movement of the plates of the Earth's crust. A volcano is a place where molten rock, called magma, comes to the surface. On land, volcanoes form where rocks have been melted underground as two plates are forced together. When such a volcano erupts, magma is pushed out of it, together with tons of ash. Once it is above ground, magma is called lava. It flows down the side of the volcano, devastating the land. Earthquakes are powerful vibrations caused by sudden movements in the Earth's crust. Most tremors are too slight to feel, but a large earthquake can destroy a city.

Submarine volcanoes

Volcanoes are found on the ocean floor as well as on land. They are called submarine volcanoes. When a submarine volcano erupts, it disturbs the ocean, and a huge tidal wave may be produced. Some tidal waves are taller than a house, and very destructive. Most submarine volcanoes are found along ocean ridges—places where two plates are being pulled apart, which makes the crust thinner, allowing magma through. The molten magma solidifies as it meets the cold water of the sea, and the sea water boils. You can imagine what happens to the fish.

Inside a volcano

Most of the time, magma is held safely inside a volcano. A volcano erupts when the magma is pushed out. In a very violent eruption, magma is forced out under great pressure, and the molten rock is shot high in the air in a series of explosions.

Earthquake!

The tectonic plates of the Earth's crust move slowly (a few inches per year), but where they collide or rub against each other, they do so with enormous force. When one plate is forced against another, vibrations are set up (imagine the noise of rubbing two heavy stones together). These massive vibrations are earthquakes and can cause great damage.

Boundary between plates

Powerful earthquakes can destroy large buildings and roads

Danger zones

Volcanoes and earthquakes occur most often along the boundary between two of the Earth's tectonic plates. Cities built near these plate boundaries are most likely to have volcanoes and earthquakes. Children who go to school in these zones have to practice earthquake drills as well as fire drills.

Some earthquake zones are in the middle of oceans, others are on land, where people live

■ Volcanoes   ■ Earthquake zones

Measuring the quake

Devices called seismographs record the vibrations of the Earth, including those during earthquakes. The seismograph in this photograph is buried under the ground. The readings are sent as radio waves by a radio transmitter, which is powered by a solar panel.

Black smoker

An underwater volcano (left) is sometimes called a black smoker, because huge plumes of black underwater smoke form where magma leaks out through the sea floor. This can kill some living creatures, while others thrive on it.

Mountain of fire

Lava does not erupt from a volcano all the time. Instead, eruptions may happen every few years or perhaps every few hundred years. As lava pours out of the top, or cone, of a volcano, it solidifies—just as hot sauce hardens as you pour over ice cream. The volcano grows each time it erupts, as more and more lava solidifies on its sides.

MAKE A SEISMOGRAPH

Inside a modern seismograph is a pendulum. You can see how this can monitor the vibrations of the Earth for yourself. Hang a weight from one end of a string, to form your pendulum's bob, and tie the other end of the string to a chair. Now, gently rock the chair to and fro, to mimic the vibrations of the Earth. The pendulum stays motionless as the chair moves. If you attach a felt-tipped pen to the bob, and place some paper beneath it, you can create a record of the vibrations.

ROCKS AND MINERALS

THE SURFACE OF THE EARTH is made up of rocks, although most of them are covered by oceans, forests, cities, rivers and hills. All rocks are made of mixtures of minerals. Different rocks have different recipes, which is why they don't look the same, and some are harder than others. Geologists can identify rocks by the minerals from which they are made. Minerals are chemicals that occur naturally, and they can be different colors such as green, brown, white, and red. Minerals are used for many purposes including cement, paint, and fuel. Some minerals are called ores and these contain metals such as copper, iron, lead, and tin. Some are pure metals, such as gold and silver. Rocks are classified into three main types—igneous, sedimentary, and metamorphic—depending on the way they were formed. Most rocks consist of crystals with regular shapes and smooth faces that grow in a symmetrical way.

Beautiful minerals

Minerals sought after for their beauty are called gemstones. Many of them are used in jewellery. Some, such as diamonds, are prized for their sparkle, or 'fire'. Others, such as rubies and emeralds, are beautifully coloured. Shown above is Chilean rhodochrozite.

Rock concert

You can often see sand or shells in sedimentary rocks. The mineral grains in igneous rocks are large if the rock is formed slowly. Metamorphic rocks, such as shale, are often flaky and brittle.

Igneous rock

Sedimentary rock

Metamorphic rock

Types of rock

Igneous rock, sometimes called fiery rock, is made from lava that has become solid either above or below the Earth's surface. Most of the Earth's crust is made of this type of rock. Sedimentary rock often covers igneous rock. It is formed by layer upon layer of soil, sand, or other small particles deposited by wind or water. These layers are squashed over millions of years and become rock. This type of rock often contains fossils and geologists use these to work out when the layers of sedimentary rock were laid down. The third rock type is called metamorphic. Its name comes from the word metamorphosis, which means transforming, or changing. This is a good name because it describes exactly what happens to the rock. The rock is changed by being heated by melted magma or by being forced together by moving plates.

A synthetic diamond made in a laboratory has the same properties as a natural diamond

Unnatural minerals

Certain useful minerals that are very rare are made, or synthesized, in laboratories. The properties of the minerals can be carefully controlled by "cooking" them at the correct temperature and pressure. These synthetic diamonds will be as hard as natural diamonds, and may be used in a drill or a cutting machine.

Under the microscope, the smallest mineral grains can be observed

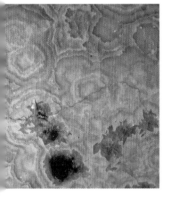

In the field

Geologists are scientists who study the rocks and minerals of the Earth. Much of their work is carried out "in the field," collecting and classifying rock samples that they study later in their laboratories.

A geologist working in the field collects rock samples by chipping away at a rock face

Rocks to order

Concrete is made with cement, which is produced by heating a rock called limestone. Once mixed with water, the concrete can be poured into molds and will set hard like a rock, to form strong, long-lasting structures such as bridges.

Out of the ground

Many rocks and minerals are obtained from deep underground, in mines like this one. A lift takes people down to the mine and carries the rocks to the surface. Some rocks are obtained from quarries, that are at ground level. In each case, explosives may be used to break the hard rocks apart.

Grainy rock

Nearly all rocks are made of countless tiny crystals, each called a grain. This close-up of a sample of the igneous rock granite shows the grains. There are three different minerals in this sample, and this explains why the grains are different colors.

The large wheel drives the lift that carries people deep underneath the ground

New rocks from old

Can you see how rocks are recycled in the Earth's crust? Igneous rocks are made from molten rock called magma, formed from rocks that have melted. Sedimentary rocks are made from bits that are worn away from other rocks. Metamorphic rocks are made from rocks that are at high temperature or under great pressure.

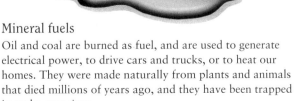

Mineral fuels

Oil and coal are burned as fuel, and are used to generate electrical power, to drive cars and trucks, or to heat our homes. They were made naturally from plants and animals that died millions of years ago, and they have been trapped in rocks ever since.

MINERAL FACTS

● Diamond is the hardest natural substance.

● The word "mineral" comes from the word "mine."

● The colors of precious stones come from "impurities," normally metal atoms.

● Quartz, used in digital watches, is the most common mineral.

ATMOSPHERE AND OCEANS

WE ARE LIVING IN A KIND OF BUBBLE: the Earth is surrounded by a mixture of gases that make up what is called the atmosphere. Beyond it is space, a hostile environment where there is no air. Life on Earth could not survive without the atmosphere. It provides us with rain and winds, and it protects us from being burned up by the Sun. The two main gases of the atmosphere are nitrogen and oxygen, but there are other gases too. The atmosphere is divided into several layers, and we live in the layer called the troposphere. This is heated by the Sun. The heat mixes the gases, dust and water in the environment, giving us weather. The oceans are in constant movement. They are affected by the Moon and the winds. Tides are caused by the gravitational pull of the Moon, which makes the sea's level rise and fall, while waves are formed by the blowing of winds across the surface of the oceans.

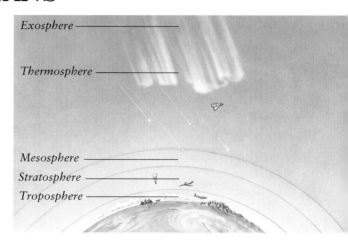

Exosphere
Thermosphere
Mesosphere
Stratosphere
Troposphere

Layers of air

At ground level, you are at the bottom of the sea of air that is the atmosphere. The atmosphere has several levels. The bottom layer, about 12 miles thick, is the troposphere. This is where nearly all our weather happens, including the clouds. The uppermost layer is the exosphere, where the air is very thin, or "rarefied." The air in the exosphere becomes more rarefied the farther up you go, until you reach space, where there is no air at all.

Journey under the sea

About two thirds of the Earth's surface is covered by oceans. Imagine a journey from one continent to another along the ocean floor. You submerge beneath the waves at the coastline, and sink gradually deeper as you move along a gentle slope called the continental shelf. Suddenly, the water becomes much deeper as you meet an underwater cliff about 650 feet into your journey. The cliff is huge—perhaps three or four miles, and you drop down to the deep ocean floor. Much of this floor is fairly flat, but in some places there are underwater mountains and volcanoes, some high enough to reach to the top of the ocean. When you are near to the other continent, the ocean floor slopes steeply upward, and you find yourself on another gently sloping continental shelf, before you finally reach the coastline.

Wave patterns

If you blow across the top of a bowl full of water, ripples appear on the water's surface. In the same way, winds that blow across the ocean's surface disturb the water, producing waves. The waves can travel great distances across the surface. They "break" when they approach the shore, where the sea is more shallow.

Deep ocean trench

Underwater mountains and volcanoes

Blue skies

Light from the Sun is white, a mixture of all colors. When it passes through the Earth's atmosphere, some of the blue light is sent in all directions. This is why a cloudless sky appears blue in whatever direction you look. The sky is always black on the Moon, because there is no atmosphere.

Have you wondered why sky without clouds is always blue?

Exploring the depths

There is no better way to find out about the bottom of the ocean than to pay it a visit. Submarines called submersibles explore the depths of the ocean. They are normally controlled from a ship at the surface.

The powerful sea

The gravitational pull of the Moon and the Sun cause the sea level to rise and fall twice every day. The rising and falling of the sea level are called tides. There is a huge amount of energy in the tides, and this can be harnessed by a tidal power station, like this one in France. The moving water works machines that generate hydroelectricity.

Air pressure

Air has weight. The weight of the air above you pushes you in all directions. This push is called pressure, and can be measured using an instrument called a barometer. One type, called an aneroid barometer, consists of a metal can attached to a needle. As the pressure increases, the can crushes more, and the needle moves up a dial.

An aneroid barometer measures atmospheric pressure

Where land meets sea

The waves that beat on the shore gradually wear away, or erode, the rocks of the shore. This erosion creates the interesting shapes of coastlines. Huge chunks of coastline may erode, leaving a rock "stack" out in the sea. Waves break up rock into smaller and smaller pieces. Sand itself is made from tiny pieces of rock that have been ground down by the waves.

The sea floor

It is a strange, dark world at the bottom of the oceans. Underwater mountains called sea mounts rise from the flat ocean floor, and in some places run long cracks in the Earth's crust called ridges. In these ridges, molten rock leaks out from the Earth's mantle and solidifies to form new rock.

SEE PRESSURE AT WORK

You can see how air pressure pushes in all directions using a plastic bottle and some warm water. Pour some of the water into the bottle and screw on the lid. As the warm air and water vapor inside the bottle cool, they take up less room, and the bottle is crushed by the pressure of the atmosphere.

JACQUES COUSTEAU

Underwater explorer Jacques Cousteau invented the aqualung, which allows divers to breathe underwater, and made many scientific discoveries in the oceans. Cousteau became well known during the 1960s and 1970s, when he made popular television programs that brought the magic of the oceans to millions of people.

Ocean ridge

WEATHER AND CLIMATES

THE EARTH HAS A HUGE VARIETY of weather. The weather affects our way of life: where we live, how we dress, what crops we grow, and what we eat. People who live in hot dry areas live very differently from those who live in cold and wet conditions, for example. Some areas have weather that stays quite similar all year, while other areas experience enormous changes from season to season. Meteorologists—scientists who study weather—work out the average weather over many years and these conditions are called climates. There are three main climates: cold, warm, and temperate, and they are all patterns of heat, water, and moving air. The Sun's heat evaporates water from oceans, making clouds. These are blown by the wind and eventually they drop rain on warm areas and snow on cold areas. The position of the Earth in relation to the Sun also affects the weather. At the South and North Poles, the Sun is always low in the sky, making it dark and very cold for much of each year.

WEATHER FACTS

● Weather forecasters use a kind of radar to chart rainfall.

● Low atmospheric pressure generally means that bad weather is on its way.

● Wind speed and strength is sometimes measured according to the Beaufort Scale, which classifies winds with numbers from 0 (calm air) to 17 (destructive hurricane).

Twister

A tornado can be devastating. Its swirling winds travel at up to 500 miles per hour. At the center of a tornado, the air shoots upward, and this can uproot trees and hurl cars into the air. The air inside the tornado is very cold, and mist forms. This is why a tornado looks like a rapidly rotating cloud.

Telling the future?

Weather watchers across the world make millions of measurements every day to keep track of temperatures and rainfall. These include information from weather satellites. If you know how the weather is one day, you can work out what it might do the next.

How air moves

If you have ever held your hand above a hot radiator, you will probably know that hot air rises. Cooler air moves into the space left behind by the warm air, and this creates a slight breeze. This circulation of air above a radiator is called a convection current, and winds are caused by convection currents. For example, during the morning, air above beaches rises. Cooler air from above the sea moves into its place, creating a gentle sea breeze. Winds do not blow in straight lines. The Earth's spin makes winds twist around in a spiral. If this spiral becomes very tight, the twisting winds blow at enormous speeds. This is a tornado. Our planet's winds mix warm and cold air together, and help to move clouds around.

Global weather

The world's weather is like a huge machine. Convection currents move air like gigantic conveyor belts around the planet. These are driven by the Sun heating up some parts of Earth more than others. Warm air picks up water from the oceans, which drops as rain or snow when warm and cold air mix.

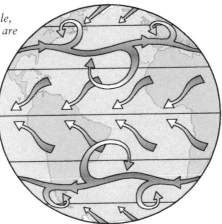

On a global scale, wind directions are determined by the spin of the Earth. Around the equator, for example, winds blow from east to west

Where in the world?

The climate of a place depends on where it is in the world. A place near the equator is normally hot, because the Sun is always high in the sky there. Climate depends on other factors too, including whether it is inland or on the coast, and its altitude.

Frozen water

When the temperature drops below 32°F, water freezes. Many clouds are made of crystals of ice, not drops of water. The ice crystals melt as they fall, to give rain. If it is below freezing at ground level, the crystals do not melt, but fall as snow.

Sea breezes

Land warms more quickly in the morning sun than water does. This is why the air above a beach becomes warmer than the air above the sea. Air from the sea moves on to the land as the warm air rises. In the evening, after the Sun goes down, the land cools more quickly than the sea, and the breeze is in the opposite direction.

Sea breezes in the morning (above) and evening (below)

What's that cloud?

Meteorologists identify clouds based on their height and appearance. Cirrus clouds are wispy and high up; stratus clouds are lower down and look like blankets of cloud. There are 10 main types of cloud.

Nimbocumulus clouds are fluffy and low, and can bring thunderstorms

Cirrocumulus are wispy and high up and are generally seen during fine weather

Cumulus clouds are fluffy clouds that can bring light rain

EARTH'S BIOSPHERE

THE PART OF THE EARTH WHERE life exists is called the biosphere. It stretches from the lower layers of the atmosphere down to the very bottom of the deepest ocean and even a few feet under the ground. The biosphere contains the complete collection of all living things, from plants and animals to fish and human beings. All of these elements are dependent upon one another and they are connected together in intricate patterns. If one part of the chain is damaged in some way, all of the other parts will be affected. Along with plants and animals, gases, and water in the atmosphere itself, as well as rocks and soil, are involved in sustaining the biosphere. Plants, for example, take water and nitrogen from the soil, energy from the Sun, and carbon dioxide from the air. They give water and oxygen to the air. Animals also use the soil and the plants themselves and these cycles are vital to sustaining life.

Living together

Different regions of the world have their own tailor-made patterns of interconnected life. These are groups of living things that are specially designed for their specific environment. The groups can be enormous. Imagine the rich variety of plants, insects, birds, and animals that inhabit a rain forest. These living things would not survive in a desert, on a mountain or in an ocean. Each of these areas has its own set of patterns and collections of living things and they are known as biomes. In each of these biome systems, there are different ecosystems—particular groups of living things that depend upon each other for their survival. Humans are also part of ecosystems and biomes.

Where in the world?

The distribution of the world's biomes is closely related to the locations of different climates. Some—such as deserts and rain forests—even have the same name. Most plants and animals that live in a particular biome would not survive long in any other biome.

- temperate deciduous forest
- savannah
- grassland
- rain forest
- chaparral (scrubby land)
- desert
- tundra
- coniferous forest

Cycles in the biosphere

All animals depend upon oxygen. They take it in, and breathe out carbon dioxide. During the day, plants take in carbon dioxide and give out oxygen. If they did not, all the oxygen in the biosphere would soon be used up, and all the animals would then die.

Emerald forest

Rain forests are found in hot, wet parts of the world, around the equator. Living things need heat and water, so the rain forest biome is home to millions of different species of plant and animal. Plants grow very quickly in the humid warmth. Trees fight for sunlight, which they need to grow. The dense layer of leaves formed by rain forest trees is called the canopy. There are many different ecosystems existing side by side in a typical rain forest.

Life in danger

Animals eat plants or other animals to survive and grow. Gorillas and orangutans (shown above) depend on the rain forest for their survival, and they have been lost in many areas where people have cut down the forest. Animals can also be hunted to extinction; the numbers of white tigers have dropped dramatically through hunting, and the animal may soon become extinct.

The mists of the forest

Water evaporates, forming water vapour, in warm weather. So, the air in a rain forest is a "saturated vapor," which means that it carries as much water as it can. This is why millions of tiny droplets of liquid water form in the air, creating the fine, wet mist that you can see.

The rain forests contain more than half of the world's living species. Many of them are now threatened with extinction. Huge forest fires in 1997 and 1998 destroyed large areas of rain forest

UNDER THREAT

● Millions of rain forest trees are cut down every day, to make paper or to clear land for building or farming. This affects millions of animals.

● Ocean ecosystems are also affected by the activities of people. The numbers of fish in the ocean has been severely reduced by overfishing.

● In the 1950s, large amounts of mercury found their way into a lake in Japan. People living in a nearby village suffered from mercury poisoning when they ate the fish.

● The animals most in danger from the activities of people are the predators, which are at the top of the food chain, because they eat other animals.

New situations

Plants and animals are adapted to living in their particular ecosystems. Human activity on our planet can create new ecosystems to which animals and plants adapt. In many parts of the world, foxes have come to rely on large cities for their supply of food.

Small world

An ecosystem can be as small as a drop of water. Several types of bacteria (microorganisms) live in this drop of water (left). They depend upon nutrients dissolved in the water. An ecosystem may be much larger, perhaps as big as a large forest or a whole desert.

EARTH IN DANGER

THE EARTH'S SIX BILLION PEOPLE are all using the planet's resources of materials and energy. As we use up these resources, we produce vast quantities of waste. These actions can disrupt the natural patterns of the biosphere, and upset the fine balances in the natural world. For example, changes to the cycles of gases in the biosphere can have far-reaching effects that people sometimes do not notice until it is too late. Scientists argue about the importance of these effects, some saying that they are terrible and others that they are really quite unimportant. But most scientists agree that humans are pumping too much carbon dioxide into the atmosphere by running cars and by polluting with factories and heavy industry. The extra carbon dioxide seems to be causing a rise of temperatures all around the world known as the enhanced greenhouse effect. This, in turn, seems to be causing sea levels to rise as the polar ice caps melt, affecting the world's climate and weather patterns.

A load of rubbish
The wrapping from the sandwich someone ate last week might be among the rubbish in this landfill site. Once the site is full, topsoil is piled on top of the rubbish. Think how much material is produced each year by the inhabitants of just one town. How much of the rubbish could have been reused or recycled?

Greenhouse effect

Burning fossil fuels, such as oil, coal, and natural gas, releases carbon dioxide into the atmosphere. Carbon dioxide is called a greenhouse gas, because it collects high in the atmosphere and traps some of the Sun's energy underneath it, like a greenhouse. This "greenhouse effect" is natural, and controls the Earth's temperature. But too much carbon dioxide in the atmosphere could lead to the Earth warming up too much. This could cause the polar ice caps to melt. Sea levels would then rise, flooding many cities. We need to use less electricity and to share public transportation to reduce the discharge of polluting gases.

Greenhouse gases

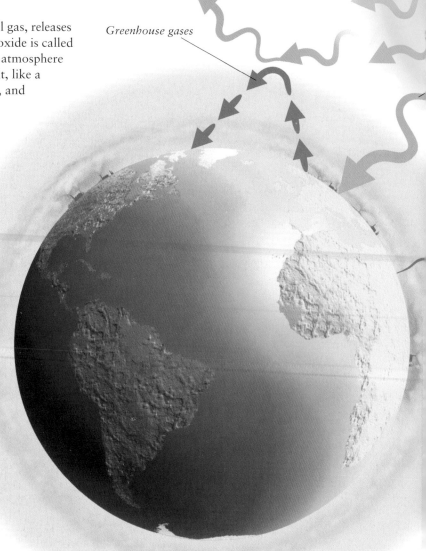

Up in smoke
Smoke and a variety of gases rise up through large factory chimneys like this one. Some of these gases can mix with water in the air and produce "acid rain," which can damage trees and other plants. Large enough amounts of gases can change the atmosphere forever.

A river of change

We throw huge quantities of bleach, shampoo, washing powders, and other substances down into the sewers every day. Some of these chemicals eventually find their way into rivers and seas, where they kill fish and other living things.

Save the planet!

It is not all bad news, though. There are ways to stop the problem getting any worse and to slow down the destruction. In most towns there are large dumpsters where people can put their household waste for recycling. Glass, paper, fabrics, tin cans, and plastic can all be crushed, washed, or melted and then used again. Most modern engineers try to design cars, household appliances, and other machines that are kinder to the environment, while manufacturers and supermarkets are under pressure to cut down on wasteful packaging. You can be an environmental activist and help to protect the Earth's resources, by being energy-efficient and by reusing or recycling things in your home and at school. You will also be doing a great job if you can tell your family and friends about ways in which they can help too.

The Sun gives out huge amounts of radiation, including ultraviolet, visible light, and infrared

The radiation from the Sun travels across 93 million miles of space, and warms the surface of the Earth

The Earth gives out infrared because it is warm. This is how it loses heat, and retains a proper temperature balance

Secondhand goods

Used glass bottles can be melted down and made into new glass. This is recycling, and many other materials can be recycled in this way. The picture shows crushed cans, newspapers, and plastic bottles packed ready to be taken to the local recycling bank. Is there a recycling bank near you?

Extra amounts of greenhouse gases such as carbon dioxide prevent some infrared from leaving the planet, making it warmer than it should be

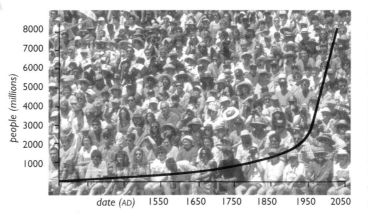

The Earth's lungs

The Earth's tropical rain forests are rich in plant and animal life. The trees produce millions of cubic feet of oxygen every day, which animals, including humans, need to survive. But humans are destroying over 30,000 square miles of rain forest every day. The wood is used for furniture and paper, while the cleared land is used for farming.

people (millions) — 8000, 7000, 6000, 5000, 4000, 3000, 2000, 1000
date (AD) 1550 1650 1750 1850 1950 2050

ECO FACTS

● The population of the world has doubled, from three billion to six billion, in the last 30 years.

● An apple core normally takes about a week to decay, while a plastic bag may take hundreds of years.

● Ozone—a naturally occurring gas in the atmosphere—protects life on Earth from the harmful effects of ultraviolet radiation. Some gases produced in factories reduce or "deplete" the amount of ozone in the atmosphere.

On the increase

The world's human population reached its first billion only 200 years ago. It now stands at around six billion, and is rising steadily. Each person needs energy and materials to live, but can the Earth cope?

Bulldozers clear many trees each day

EVOLUTION

FOR AS LONG AS THERE have been people on Earth, there have been questions about how and why life exists as it does. Many different ideas and explanations have been suggested over the years. Scientists have shown that the idea known as evolution is the best explanation. They have proved that the idea works by looking at fossils and by studying the way in which animals and plants adapt themselves to changes in their environments. Animals and plants that are well suited to their environment will survive best and pass on their characteristics to the following generations. Groups of plants or animals that share similar features are a kind of family, known as a species. Scientists can look backward into history and show that all species come from the same ancient parents. Each living thing is a blend of older and newer features, and each species is always developing and adapting, and this branching out looks rather like an enormous and complicated family tree.

Looking back

Older sedimentary rocks are lower than the later ones, because they were laid down first, and so digging down into the rocks is like looking back through geological history. Most plant and animal remains are lost forever when they die, because their bodies decay, but some are preserved in sedimentary rocks. By studying these fossils of animals and plants, scientists have been able to trace the evolution of many species.

Hairs kept the mammoth warm in the cold conditions in which it lived

Natural selection

The peppered moth spends much of its time on tree trunks. Its wings are light gray and look like small pieces of the trees' bark. This hides them from predators such as birds. In industrial areas during the 19th century, the bark of trees became darker with smoke and other pollution. This made the moths stand out against the bark, and many more were eaten by the birds. A small proportion of the moths were darker gray, so they were safer resting on the polluted tree bark. More of these moths survived, passing their darker colouring on to the next generations. Gradually the whole species has changed to have darker coloring. This process is called natural selection, and it is one of the main ideas in the theory of evolution.

CHARLES DARWIN

The English naturalist Charles Darwin (1809-1882) developed his ideas about evolution into a proper scientific theory. His book *The Origin of Species*, published in 1859, explained the principle of natural selection.

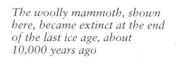

Reaching up and down

People have long wondered how the giraffe got its long neck. Fossils show that ancient ancestors of the giraffe had much shorter necks and shorter legs. Over millions of years, giraffes' legs grew longer, so that they could reach leaves higher in the trees. People think that the neck grew longer too, so that giraffes could still reach down to drink water.

The woolly mammoth, shown here, became extinct at the end of the last ice age, about 10,000 years ago

Genetics

Once the idea of evolution was accepted, scientists began to wonder how characteristics of animals, such as their coloring, could be passed from generation to generation. This is called inheritance. The rules of inheritance were worked out, and were named "genetics." The key to genetics lies in a chemical called DNA (deoxyribonucleic acid), found in all living things. Your DNA is like a blueprint for your body, and is unique to you. When a man and a woman have a baby, the baby's DNA comes from the mother and the father, and this is how characteristics such as eye color and hair color are passed on. Members of a species that are successful and produce offspring pass on their DNA, and so their characteristics, to the next generation.

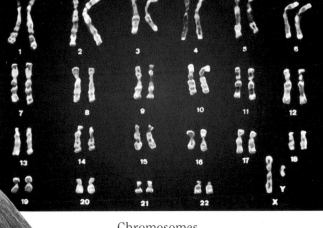

This diagram shows the shape of a DNA molecule—a double helix

DNA is found in the nucleus of every cell in your body

Information is carried along the length of DNA

Dead and gone

As plant and animal species evolve, they develop. This change means that each year some species become extinct, and most fossils are of plants and animals that have already been extinct for millions of years.

Chromosomes

The DNA inside cells of a living thing is found in lengths called chromosomes. Every human being has 46 chromosomes, in 23 pairs. One member of each pair comes from each parent. Chromosomes can be photographed under a microscope, and the photograph manipulated to show the chromosomes in a standard arrangement called a karyotype. This karyotype is of a male human being.

EVOLUTION FACTS

● Identical twins have exactly the same information in their DNA.

● The "human genome project," begun in 1990, is an international effort to decode the information in human DNA. It will be finished in 2005.

● Mistakes in the copying of DNA from one generation to the next are called mutations.

● Life on Earth seems to have begun around 3. 5 billion years ago, as simple one-celled organisms in the sea.

● Human beings evolved from apes, about three million years ago.

FOSSILS AND DINOSAURS

*Head at a
height of about
40 feet*

Great collectors

Paleontologists are always
hunting for ever more fossils.
Some do this just for fun, or to
make collections, but others study
fossils hoping to discover how long-extinct
animals lived, or what ancient species of plants looked like.
Most fossil collections contain ammonites. These were
creatures that lived between 408 million and 66 million years
ago. Fossils of these animals are commonly found in
sedimentary rock that formed at the sea bed. A modern
animal, the pearly nautilus, is a descendant of the ammonite.

FOSSILS ARE
PRODUCED over
millions of years as
sedimentary rocks form in
layers around dead animals,
plants, and insects. The layers help
paleontologists—people who study
fossils—to work out when the plant or
animal lived. In some cases, bones are
preserved in a fossil, but mostly, minerals from
the rocks filled the gaps that the plant or animal
made when it decayed. Either way, a solid imprint
forms in the rocks, and that is a fossil. Plants can become
fossils only if they were buried in soil and flattened quickly,
otherwise they decay before a fossil imprint can be made. Among
the best fossils are those of shellfish. Because they lived and died
under water, they were fossilized before they had a chance to decay.

*Brachiosaurus lived in
Africa, North America,
and Europe*

Terrible lizards

Dinosaurs—the word means "terrible lizards"—were one of
the most successful species ever to have lived on Earth. We
know about their lives through their fossilized remains. They
were reptiles, the first animals that could survive well on
land. By matching dinosaur fossils with the calendar of the
Earth's history that the layers of rock have given us,
paleontologists have decided that dinosaurs were wiped out
in a mass extinction around 65 million years ago.

> ### DINOSAUR FACTS
>
> There are two orders of
> dinosaurs: Ornithischia
> and Saurischia.
>
> ● Ornithischia all evolved
> from a single species.
>
> ● Saurischia do not come
> from a common ancestor.

*Stegosaurus, like
other dinosaurs,
had dry, scaly skin*

Why did dinosaurs become extinct?

Many paleontologists believe that around 65 million years ago a
large meteorite hit the Earth. The impact is thought to have caused
climate changes that killed vegetation and destroyed much of the
dinosaurs' food. With such a shock to the environment the
dinosaurs could no longer survive.

Jurassic Park

Some small animals have been
preserved in fossilized tree
sap, called amber. This
insect may have fed off
a dinosaur's blood.

Animal dies

Soft parts rot

Minerals fill the space of the soft body parts

How fossils are formed

When an animal or plant dies, it falls on to the sand under the sea or into mud or sand on the land. The soft parts rot, but hard parts such as bones and teeth do not. Sedimentary rocks form from sediment around the remains of the animal or plant. The hard parts of the skeleton are gradually replaced over millions of years by minerals from the rock-forming sediment.

Fossil

The dimetrodon was like a modern lizard, but could grow to be 3.5 metres long.

Large lizard

The Dimetrodon was a large reptile with a distinctive smile, which lived before the dinosaurs, around 250 million years ago. The sharp teeth show that it was a predator, and the sail on its back may have been used to control the body temperature, in the same way that an elephant uses its ears today.

Strong legs supported the weight of the brachiosaurus, which probably spent most of its time in water

Feathers like modern birds

Shape like a small dinosaur

Early bird

A peculiar dinosaur was archaeopteryx. This artist's impression was worked out from fossils of the species. Some people think it is a "missing link" in evolution, between dinosaurs and birds. Archaeopteryx lived between about 160 and 140 million years ago, and was typically the size of a large chicken. Studies of the arrangement of its feathers indicate that it could probably fly.

A fiery end?

This is a massive crater at Chicxulub, in Mexico. A huge fireball, a comet or meteor from space, hit the Earth there 65 million years ago, and may have been the main cause of the extinction of the dinosaurs.

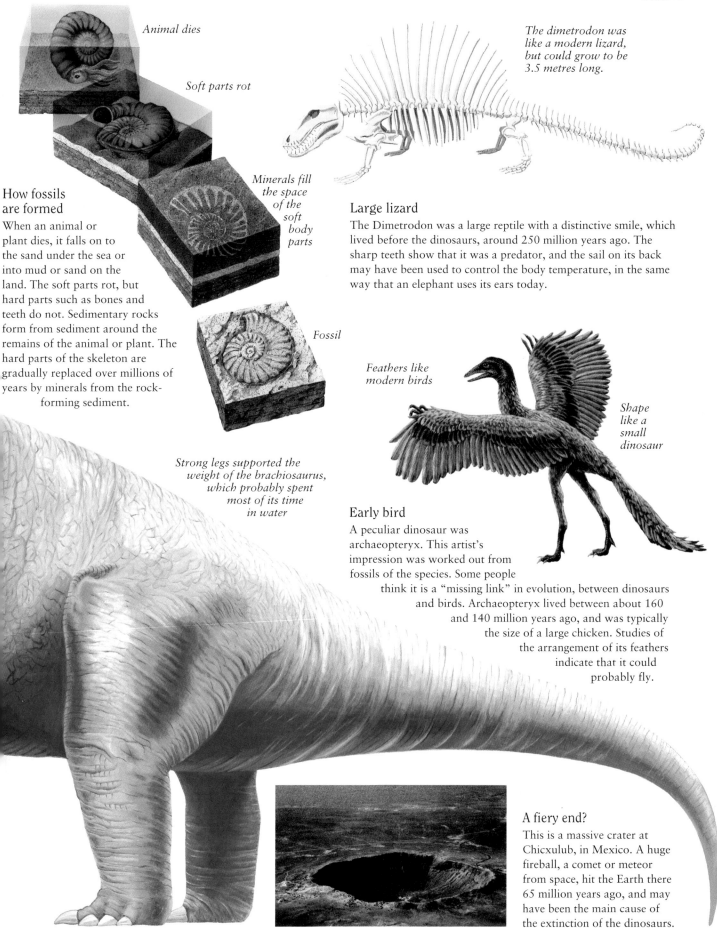

THE FIRST HUMANS

HUMAN BEINGS HAVE BEEN LIVING on Earth for millions of years, and like all other living things our development has been affected by the process of evolution. Paleontologists have used fossil evidence to discover information about our ancestors. The earliest fossils have mainly been found in Africa and show how we have evolved from apes. The family that includes humans and some apes is called Hominids and first appeared on Earth around three million years ago. Modern humans—a species called Homo sapiens—are descended from these early Hominids. As they developed, their brain size increased, the skull became higher and the face flatter. Earlier Homo sapiens had a similar appearance to us, but with a prominent forehead and a sloping skull. In recent years, scientists have been able to use new technologies to show that human DNA is almost identical to other creatures in the Hominid family. Gradually, over the past 500,000 years, humans have learned to make and use fire, farm the land, and eventually to live in permanent settlements.

Home sweet home

Olduvai Gorge in northern Tanzania, Africa, is one of the richest sites of for fossils of early Hominids. As many as 50 Hominid specimens, dating as far back as four million years, have been found here, along with evidence of primitive tools and shelters.

Hunter-gatherers

Early humans wandered from place to place, gathering fruits and berries, and hunting animals to eat. It was not until about 10,000 years ago that humans started to settle and farm their food. This artist's impression shows a group of European hunter-gatherers. They have made their own shelters and are using fire to cook and keep warm. The first real city was still a long way off. It was not built until about 8,000 years ago.

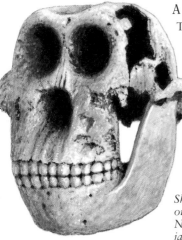

A direct link?

The jaws and teeth of Ramapithicus, that lived between eight and 15 million years ago, are more similar to those of modern humans than to apes. This has led experts to suggest that Ramapithicus is a missing link in the evolution of apes to humans.

Skull of Ramapithicus, our ancient ancestor. Note the heavy apelike jaw

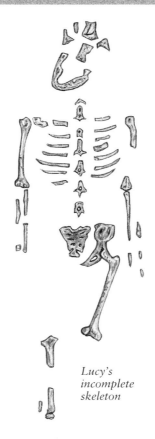

Lucy's incomplete skeleton

Old woman

In the 1970s and 1980s, many fossils of early humans were discovered in a small region of Ethiopia, Africa. One of the fossils was given the official name AL 288-1, but she was affectionately called "Lucy." The fossilized bones are about four million years old.

Old man

More and more skeletons of early humans are found every year, and together they help to piece together the story of evolution from apes to humans.

The first Hominids to walk upright were Homo erectus. This is a computer-generated picture showing what Homo erectus looked like.

Homo erectus lived around 800,000 years ago

Family tree

Some of the earliest humans were called Homo habilis and there is evidence that they used tools and hunted. They made hand axes and other tools from stone and these have been found in Africa, along with fossil evidence of the species. Fossils of a more recent ancestor, Homo erectus, have been found in Southeast Asia as well as in Africa, suggesting population growth. One form of Homo sapiens was called Neanderthal Man and looked very similar to modern day humans. This branch of the family is thought to have existed about 200,000 years ago. It is possible that the species died out completely, or that the Neanderthal people bred with another form of Homo sapiens. These early humans showed signs of social organization. It has been shown, for example, that they had special places where they buried people.

First light

Humans have been around for several million years, but it was only about half a million years ago—when they lived in caves to shelter from the weather and wild animals—that they discovered how to make fires and use them for heating and lighting. More recently, people used fires for cooking, and—as recently as 4,000 years ago—for smelting metals from ores.

The right tools

Homo sapiens is among very few animal species that make and use tools. Early humans made tools from a hard mineral called flint. They chipped away at pieces of flint to make a sharp edge, which could be used as a knife, an arrowhead, or attached to a piece of wood as an ax.

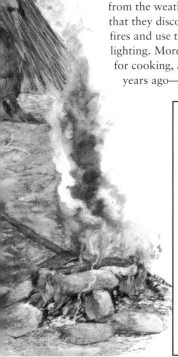

HOMINID FACTS

● The oldest known Hominid species is Ardipithicus ramidus. It is dated at 4.4 million years.

● Homo habilis was probably the first Hominid with the ability to speak. Its skull has a bulge in the brain in a position related to our ability to talk.

● The name for modern humans is Homo sapiens sapiens. Our species, Homo sapiens, appeared more than 100,000 years ago.

Big heads

These pictures show how the shape and size of the skull changed as humans evolved from apes. The ape's skull is smaller, and with a flatter forehead. The modern human has a much larger space for his or her brain.

INDEX

ACKNOWLEDGMENTS

The publishers wish to thank the following artists who have contributed to this book:

Mike Atkinson; Julian Baker; Andrew Farmer; Jeremy Gower; Gary Hincks; Richard Hook; Rob Jakeway; Kuo Kang Chen; Alan Male; Janos Marff;, Mel Pickering; Terry Riley; Peter Sarson; Guy Smith; Roger Smith; Sue Stitt; Stephen Sweet; Darrell Warner; Mike White

The publishers wish to thank the following for supplying photographs for this book:

Page 11 (B/R) NASA; 12 (B/R) NASA; 15 (C,C/R) NASA; 17 (C/R) NASA; 18 (B/L) Gamma/Frank Spooner Pictures, (B/R) NASA; 21 (C/L) David Parker/Science Photo Library, (C/R) David A. Hardy/Science Photo Library; 23 (C/R) Martin F. Chillmaid/Oxford Scientific Films; 28 (C) Colin Milkins/Oxford Scientific Films; 29 (T/R) Robin Redfern/Oxford Scientific Films; 36 (T/R) John Reader/Science Photo Library; 37 (C/R) John Reader/Science Photo Library

All other photographs from Miles Kelly archives.